"He's lucky! If his Socialist paradise is a disaster, he's rich enough to go and live in America!"

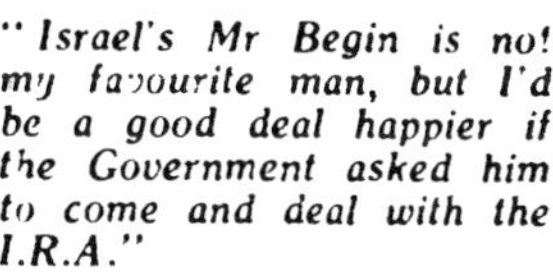

"Israel's Mr Begin is not my favourite man, but I'd be a good deal happier if the Government asked him to come and deal with the I.R.A."

"Dont jump! The rumour that Harold Wilson's been called back to save the nation is quite untrue!"

"With us it's not a question of: 'Will the President manage to finish his second term?' But, 'Will Comrade Chernenko manage to finish his first speech?'."

"Sorry, Sir! I got caught in the cross-fire between a bombardment of French Golden Delicious and a counter-attack of English Cox's Orange Pippins."

"The only snag about lying down, Doris, is that it might make male chauvinist judges think we're encouraging rape."

"Don't let that Russian know that Scargill wants to take over the country, or he might re-defect back to Moscow."

"How convenient! When we rob the banks that are shut on Saturday we can bank the loot in the bank that's open on Saturday."

On the Point of my Pen

The Best of Cummings

Michael Cummings

Milestone Publications

© Michael Cummings/Express Newspapers plc 1985

All rights reserved. No part of this publication may be reproduced, stored in a retrieval system, or transmitted in any form, or by any means, whether electronic, mechanical, photocopying, recording or otherwise, without the prior permission of the author except for brief passages in criticism or review.

Published by
Milestone Publications
62 Murray Road
Horndean
Portsmouth Hants PO8 9JL

British Library Cataloguing in Publication Data
Cummings, Michael
On the point of my pen : the best of Cummings.
1. English wit and humor, Pictorial
I. Title
741.5'942 NC1479

ISBN 0 903852 69 1

Typeset by Inforum, Portsmouth
Printed and bound in Great Britain by
R J Acford, Chichester, Sussex

Contents

THATCHER RULES . . . ER . . . O.K! 9

Britannia takes on the job of trying to rule the waves of lethargy, stubbornness, old-fashioned ideas, bloody-mindedness and woolly thinking that wash over the island and have kept it wet so long. De Gaulle once said in a moment of despair about France: 'How can one govern a country with 257 different kinds of cheese!' Thatcher might well say: 'How can I govern a country with 257 different kinds of political dinosaurs!'

THE ROYAL FAMILY 68

Once regarded as so sacrosanct that no newspaper cartoonist ever dared draw them. But now objects of such endless fascination that no comedian, cartoonist or puppet-maker can bear to leave them alone.

BY THE LEFT, QUICK MARCH! 78

The Party whose demented writhings brings it ever more into the clutches of political loonies and "sane" Marxists, makes one weep rather than laugh.

DIVIDED BY THE SAME LANGUAGE 118

Would we be happier to be the 52nd state of the U.S.A.? But the land of the ex-colonists that speaks English, feels more like a foreign country than the Europe that speaks French, German, Italian or Spanish.

WITH LOVE FROM RUSSIA 131

Russia - like Hitler's Germany - is a spectacle not for those of a nervous disposition.

THE ENTENTE DISCORDIALE 152

Our fascinating, alluring and maddening next door neighbour who we think of as the best of enemies or the worst of friends.

ABROAD "I DON'T LIKE ABROAD!" . . . GEORGE V 167

Where live the Irish, The Third World, the blacks, the browns and the yellows whom we thank God we aren't still ruling.

THE PERMISSIVE SOCIETY 194

The society once hailed by S.D.P. politician, Roy Jenkins, as "the civilised society" becomes beyond a joke, though the humorist still tries to make one.

SEA OF TROUBLES 217

Persecuted by the unions, ousted by the woman, Thatcher, perhaps its unkind to intrude on private grief. Alas, poor Heath!

DOWN MEMORY LANE 233

Distance lends enchantment to the view of an elder statesman. The greater the number of years you are away from a Prime Minister's retirement, the lovelier he looks. - particularly if he is Harold Macmillan.

Introduction

People always wonder why political cartoonists become cartoonists and how they produce their cartoons.

My father was a political journalist, and my first political experience was when he took me on a picnic with David Lloyd George, since when I have always been interested in politics. Thus, with this Liberal background I subsequently earned my first cheque signed by the formidable Socialist, Sir Stafford Cripps, for a cartoon published in his paper, the *Tribune*. Later, this weekly was edited by Michael Foot, who encouraged me to draw cartoons for him. I doubt whether the ultimate fruits of this early encouragement pleased him.

When I wrote to Lord Beaverbrook for a job on the Express Group, he sent me a charming letter in reply explaining that "he was just an old man who now had nothing to do with the papers and spent his days in the sun" but giving me an appointment to see Arthur Christiansen, the editor of the *Daily Express*. I was engaged as the political cartoonist.

Beaverbrook, however, gave no signs of being an old man spending his days in the sun, but kept an eagle eye on all I did. He frequently disagreed with my political views and summoned me to lunches and dinners to tell me why. Sometimes he found me too critical of the Tories - particularly in the last year of Macmillan's government. But he never stopped a cartoon from being published because he disagreed with it.

Cartoonists can't please all the people all the time. I've been accused of being anti-American, anti-French, anti-German, anti-British, anti-Russian, anti-Labour, anti-Tory, anti-Liberal, anti-coloured, anti-white, anti-good taste, anti-Royal Family and anti-trade union. In spite of this, many politicians, trade unionists, members of the Royal Family and Prime Ministers have asked for the originals of the cartoons that depict them. I remember a remark made to me by Emanuel Shinwell early in my career: "My boy, however angry politicians may be by the way you draw them in your cartoons, they'll be more angry if you leave them out!"

One of the most controversial politicians has been Enoch Powell. When he made his "rivers of blood" speech attacking immigration, I drew a cartoon suggesting that what he said was what most people were thinking. I received over two hundred letters from readers congratulating me on the cartoon.

Some months later Powell made a speech suggesting repatriation for immigrants. For this, I did a cartoon showing Macmillan being repatriated to Scotland and the Royal Family being repatriated to its origins in Germany. This cartoon provoked over a hundred letters from irate readers for daring to mock the words of Saint Enoch.

The politicians who appear most frequently in cartoons are those with the most striking features. Harold Wilson was almost never drawn before he became Leader of the Labour Party, because his face had about as much variety as the underside of a soup plate. I enjoyed drawing him only when I discovered the bags under his eyes, which I developed so enthusiastically that I could make him recognisable by simply drawing a round shape with two bags like prunes plus a pipe. Kinnock has an equally evasive face, his only outstanding features being his freckles. What cartoonists love are the wild, staring eyes of Benn, the eyebrows of Healey, the nose of de Gaulle, the drooping eyes of Macmillan and the bemused hair of Foot - though Foot's appearance was so grotesque that the art of caricature could scarcely improve on nature.

It is said that politicians grow to look like their caricatures. I'm convinced that one politician - Sir Gerald Nabarro - grew and nourished his monumental moustache purely for the caricaturists. Once I drew it in a way he did not like and he telephoned me, peremptorily, never to use the offending drawing again.

Another politician who was sensitive about the way I had drawn him was Labour Party Leader, Hugh Gaitskell. At a Party conference he once approached me with a charming smile and outstretched hand saying I was the only person among a group of journalists he did not know. When I told him my name his smile was extinguished, his hand withdrawn, he turned his back and abruptly marched upstairs to his hotel room.

The French government under de Gaulle was also sensitive to cartoons, and the Quai d'Orsay once officially protested to the British Foreign Office about a cartoon of de Gaulle I had done.

At that time the Entente Discordiale was particularly discordiale and the French government clearly believed I had produced an especially offensive drawing on the instructions of Prime Minister Macmillan.

Shortly after this episode, I was asked to draw a special cartoon of de Gaulle for a French weekly paper. But the Editor was terrified I was going to make the President's nose too long. Every half hour there was a telephone call to urge me to make the nose shorter, so the end result may have displeased the great man for failing to do justice to his face.

I'm often asked how I think up ideas for cartoons. But the world today is so mad that there's no shortage of subjects. For example, the Loony Left in this country is so loony that its activities are nearly beyond caricature and make cartoonists feel redundant.

I'm also asked how long it takes to produce a cartoon. I usually get up in the morning at 7 o'clock, and listen to the news and features on Radio 4 while I'm shaving and dressing. I read the papers after breakfast and by the time I get to the office I've thought out various ideas. I then rough out these ideas in pencil. At mid-day I show five or six of these drawings - some with captions and some that don't need captions - to the Editor. He picks the one he likes best or he may pick two and ask me which one I like best. The artist is not always the best judge of his own work, so usually I'm satisfied with the selection the editor makes.

When my idea has been selected, I draw the cartoon carefully in ink. The original cartoon is four times the size of the reproduction size published on the paper's page. This part of the work can take three hours to six hours, depending on the amount of elaboration. A picture showing the inside of the House of Commons packed with turbulent politicians takes much longer than one of Mrs. Thatcher dressed as Britannia with a trophy on the tip of her trident. I can, though, speed up the whole process in an emergency.

People are surprised to hear that cartoons can take so long to draw. Cartooning is rather like cooking. The chef takes hours to produce an elaborate dish with elaborate sauces - but which is eaten in fifteen minutes. A cartoon takes hours to produce and is looked at for fifteen seconds.

However, a cartoon can deliver its message in a flash, whereas a leading article needs ten minutes reading to get its political message delivered. In the following pages some messages will be delivered - hopefully, in a flash!

‘Thatcher rules . . . er . . . OK!’

"Time we modernised OUR image! Perhaps I'd better change my sex at once!"

Margaret Thatcher elected Leader of the Tory Party

13 February, 1975

"Oh no, we can't allow it to land on the Opposition Front Bench—it's so noisy it might wake up Reggie."

Mr Reggie Maudling, the Shadow Home Secretary, had a reputation for taking his duties in a very relaxed fashion

17 January, 1976

"HE'S THE FATHER!"

27 February, 1976

The new leader of the Tory Party and the old leader of the Tory Party find it difficult to adjust to each other

8 October, 1976

"Judging by the state of the Nation, Shirley Williams, it's perfectly clear that the weaker sex has NEVER mastered the three Rs..."

15 October, 1976

1 November, 1978

"St John-Stevas — get a clothes brush! Howe — get your hair cut! Whitelaw — find a decent tailor! Heseltine — use a lawn mower! Prior — get your trousers pressed! And then we can start redecorating the country!"

17 May, 1979

"You must be a VERY Iron Lady! You're the only member of the Cabinet who can look into the crystal ball without fainting!"

10 October, 1979

"We all know, Maggie, that women can bear pain better than men—but you look as if you ENJOY it!"

2 November, 1979

'I wish I was an Iron Lady powerful enough to transfer the Trade Union Olympics to Moscow'

Bill Sirs was conducting a strike against the Steel Corporation headed by Sir Charles Villiers. The water men's union was threatening a strike and other unions were rumbling with discontents to come

18 January, 1980

FRONT OF BRASS AND FEET OF CLAY

James Prior was charged with drawing up legislation to curb the power of the unions, a task he undertook with diffidence and hesitation

6 February, 1980

"Finding it difficult to drive, Mrs Thatcher? You should accept our advice – we have UNRIVALLED experience of driving!"

22 February, 1980

The Tory "wets" try to inundate the Prime Minister. *Morning Cloud* was the name of Heath's yacht

10 February, 1980

"Good morning, my Rt. Hon. Moderate Colleagues! Are there any more great moderate triumphs to report today?"

5 March, 1980

"This is a frightfully rough sea, Mrs Thatcher! Wouldn't it be safer to return to the Titanic?"

16 March, 1980

"This is frightful, Lord Carrington! How can you expect a grocer's daughter to understand our distinguished traditions!"

23 March, 1980

Len Murray – the face that launched the Day of Protest political strike against Mrs Thatcher's policies

16 April, 1980

30 April, 1980

The Labour opposition was in a state of depression, strife and demoralisation

23 May, 1980

"I'm afraid, darling, my other half doesn't understand me!"

Mr Prior seemed more concerned to placate the unions than his boss

9 July, 1980

STARTED BY ADAM AND EVE (AND STIRRED UP BY ANNA FORD)

"What! Has she the nerve to suggest I was chosen for my looks and not because I know everything better than anyone else!"

11 July, 1980

"Mrs Thatcher! Why don't you simply abolish the laws of gravity?"

3 September, 1980

"The shame! The disgrace! Illegitimate!

27 March, 1981

"Even better, let us take over! After all, we've unrivalled knowledge of the problems – we invented them!"

19 November, 1980

Mrs Thatcher was being urged to navigate on the rocks of the old reflationary policies that had proved to be disastrous

23 November, 1980

"There aren't enough women in my cabinet!"

7 April, 1982

The Foreign Office ministers were in disgrace for being taken by surprise over the invasion of the Falklands by Argentina, Defence Minister Nott for encouraging the Argentines by withdrawing a naval ship from the Falklands area, Home Secretary Whitelaw for being too lethargic at the Home Office and Employment Secretary Prior for dragging his feet over legislation for curbing trade union power

The task force to recover the Falklands sails from Britain

16 April, 1982

"Actually, I'm having the greatest difficulty in maintaining British sovereignty over **BRITAIN**!"

Riots break out in Britain

23 April, 1982

"Bad luck, President Galtieri! We didn't think the British would fight either!"

25 April, 1982

"Admiral! World opinion will support us if we only attack the Argentine navy with that, and they also promise to come to our funeral"

The world did not approve of the Navy behaving like a navy by sinking the Belgrano, and H.M.S. Sheffield was sunk by an Exocet missile

7 May, 1982

"Members of the crew! An Argentinian missile approaches!
We will have an emergency debate to discuss whether we shoot it down!"

19 May, 1982

23 May, 1982

"Shocking! Someone's written a dirty word!"

30 May, 1982

British security measures, whether at Buckingham Palace or our defence organisations, are no better under Thatcherism than under previous governments

18 July, 1982

"If you know of a better hole, Dean, lead me to it . . ."

There is a gigantic row about how the service of thanksgiving for victory in the Falklands at St Paul's Cathedral should be conducted

28 July, 1982

"Mind you, we'd have been delighted to celebrate a victory parade which was a teeny bit different..."

13 October, 1982

"Man? I'm actually described as a MAN! I've never been so insulted in all my life!"

12 January, 1983

"In this establishment only women are allowed at the bar, and men will only get the drink that's good for them!"

President Reagan was in disgrace for his "even-handed" approach during the Falklands war

10 November, 1982

1 July, 1983

"It's the burden of NOT having the burden of office that exhausts me, Mrs Thatcher!"

Mr Steel went into temporary retirement because he was fatigued by the ardours of general electioneeing

8 July, 1983

"**Emergency**! The other waxworks have got so hot under the collar at having to share the same room with him that they've melted!"

29 July, 1983

Mrs Thatcher has an eye operation and has to wear a patch **7 August, 1983**

20 August, 1983

Another Tory sex scandal is unveiled by Cecil Parkinson's mistress

16 October, 1983

Miss Tisdall, a civil servant, sends the secrets of the arrival time of Cruise missiles at Greenham Common to a newspaper and is sentenced to six months' imprisonment

30 March, 1984

Organised violence by Scargill's pickets reaches a level of brutal intimidation never seen before in this country

3 June, 1984

"My God! Has this developed from me?"

1 July, 1984

Mr Scargill's picket army is deployed to prevent fuel for the steel industry getting to the steel works

4 July, 1984

"I want to propose an Emergency Resolution — I'd like to ask Mr Scargill's permission to go to the W.C."

30 September, 1984

"The Bishop of Durham may not believe in miracles, but I do!"

Dr Jenkins casts doubt on the story of the Virgin Birth and the Resurrection but not on his faith in the miners' cause

23 September, 1984

The I.R.A. blows up the hotel where the Government stayed at the Tories' Brighton conference

14 October, 1984

Neil Kinnock is embarrassed when Scargill asks Colonel Kadhafi for money to help the miners' strike

7 November, 1984

Scargill appears to be losing his strike

16 November, 1984

28 November, 1984

Two miners' pickets drop a concrete slab on a taxi carrying a working miner, which kills the taxi driver

2 December, 1984

7 December, 1984

20 January, 1985

30 January, 1985

'The Royal Family'

"Is there any truth, Your Highness, in the rumour that you are going to build a mini-palace with all the bricks you've dropped?"

George Brown, the colourful Foreign Secretary and dropper of so many engaging clangers, meets a rival for the award of Brick-dropper in Chief

12 November, 1969

"Just think how it would help our tourist trade if Queen Elizabeth got fed up with Britain and emigrated to MY country!"

17 February, 1975

"As the only nationalised industry that makes a fortune, why not get Her Majesty to celebrate her Jubilee EVERY year?"

7 June, 1977

"I love red—but NOT red carpets!"

31 July, 1981

"With a Home Secretary like me she needs ALL the help the Almighty can give her..."

The day an intruder broke into Buckingham Palace, wandered along the corridors and into the Queen's bedroom, sat on her bed and conversed with her about his problems

14 July, 1982

"That bang, Mr Whitelaw? Not to worry, it's probably the Queen's Daimler backfiring in the Palace courtyard"

The deficient level of security at the Palace caused amazement

16 July, 1982

"I think someone's made an unauthorised entry into Mr Whitelaw's room and has wakened him up!"

There was widespread lack of confidence in Mr Whitelaw's measures for preventing further trespassers into Buckingham Palace

17 July, 1982

"Ambulance! Come quickly! Mr Whitelaw has fainted with the shock of GOOD news!"

After the Royal intrusion scandal, Commander Trestrail, in charge of Royal security, is revealed as a homosexual and resigns

30 July, 1982

Prince Andrew goes out with a doctor's daughter, Mark Thatcher goes out with a millionaire's daughter

22 February, 1984

‘By the Left, quick march!’

Mr Rising Price was invented during the election campaign of 1951 which brought the Tories under Winston Churchill's leadership back to power. The Editor suggested I invent a symbol for something that worried everybody, which, he informed me, was the constant rise in the cost of living. As a bachelor at that time, I was unaware that such a phenomenon as rising prices existed, but I soon learned my lesson, and the unlovely figure of Mr Rising Price has been stalking through my cartoons ever since

26 January, 1966

Frank Cousins, the head on the top of the staff, was the radical left wing leader in charge of the Transport Union who used the union as a formidable pressure group brought to bear on Labour governments

11 July, 1966

"Little man! Take me to your leader!"

Russian Prime Minister Kosygin arrives in Britain

6 February, 1967

"My kingdom! My kingdom for a gimmick!"

24 July, 1967

"What's so cheering about looking at the Liberals is that you suddenly realise there is something worse than Harold Wilson..."

The unhappy Jeremy Thorpe presided over a party with a bewildering variety of bizarre and extreme views, particularly among the Young Liberals

22 September, 1967

"I'm not here to arrest you—I'm here to thank you for paying me the compliment that you actually want to LIVE in a country I'm in charge of"

8 January, 1968

"There's a bad case of haunting around here, Archbishop, and I need a dynamic exorcism at once!"

2 February, 1968

As usual, the politicians did nothing really effective about the crime wave **13 February, 1970**

"Bad? Oh no, my dear, we're good in parts!"

8 June, 1970

Mr Wilson's attitude to the Common Market was not yet clear

5 July, 1971

13 December, 1972

"Mr. Wilson! Is there any truth in the scandal rumour that Wedgwood Benn is a secret Tory hired by Mr. Heath to ruin Labour's image?"

The extreme views of Benn were felt by the Party leaders to be damaging the image of Labour

11 May, 1973

Wilson's referendum on joining the Common Market is won by an overwhelming "Yes" vote

7 June, 1975

"Excuse me, Big Brother, but I think Big Daddy is about to withdraw his labour"

Yet another financial crisis

29 June, 1975

'Fortunately, the little grey cells of your Hercule Poirot have been trying to solve this case for only 22 months!"

Agatha Christie's *Murder on the Orient Express* was made into an enormously-popular film

14 January, 1976

"I hope you realise, Healey, that if that dangerous egalitarian Foot becomes Prime Minister he may confiscate all our second homes!"

28 March, 1976

"Of course I'm looking relaxed—I'M only the Prime Minister!"

7 April, 1976

"Gosh! I wish I had the courage of Mr. Healey's convictions!"

The pound collapses, Healey turns back from catching a plane at Heathrow in panic and the International Monetary Fund is called in to run our financial affairs

4 June, 1976

"No, I'm afraid you can't pay your bill with a copy of the Labour Party Manifesto..."

The Labour Party conference at Blackpool was taking place

29 September, 1976

"Heath is lucky! It's the orchestra who's conducting ME . . ."

Mr Callaghan is referring to Edward Heath, the distinguished music lover and conductor

24 November, 1976

"I can assure you—there are no Reds UNDER the bed!"

7 May, 1978

THE EMPTIES

14 May, 1978

"In order to restore the popularity ratings and the dignity of Parliament, I have introduced some new talent to the Commons..."

The Government was becoming very unpopular, and the Muppets Show became wildly popular

8 June, 1978

"My new 'Exams-without-tears' have been a brilliant success. Our engineers and designers all passed with flying colours!"

Mrs Shirley Williams was occupying the position of what was euphemistically called the Minister of "Education"

25 October, 1978

"Jim! NUPE have now given you permission to jump if you want to! They've authorised the grave diggers to work in special cases!"

Part of the famous winter of discontent when everybody seemed to be on strike and the Labour Party's union supporters did so much to ensure their Government was thrown out of office

4 February, 1979

"What we need is a law forbidding the fitting of tachographs to politicians!"

The tachograph, which was opposed by the unions, was a device fitted to lorries to monitor the performance of the drivers.

9 March, 1979

"...and of course, dear, you won't mind my family living with us!"

With a general election in prospect, Mr Callaghan woos the nation

11 April, 1979

"Mr Benn! You have assaulted my mother, murdered my children, burnt down my home! But be careful you don't go too far—or I'll write something nasty about you in my memoirs!"

Mr Benn makes life difficult for the leader of his party

28 October, 1979

The future leaders of the S.D.P. were agonising about the direction the Party was taking

3 August, 1980

10 September, 1980

A rallying call from the new Leader of the Labour Party

16 November, 1980

"By the very left, by the left, by the centre—quick march!"

The Social Democrat Liberal Alliance enjoys an embarrassment of richly-different viewpoints

2 April, 1982

"It's all very well putting the boot in—but will I ever be able to get it out again?"

Michael Foot attempts to deal with the militant Left

29 September, 1982

The remains of Henry VIII's warship the *Mary Rose* were salvaged from the depths of the sea off Portsmouth

3 October, 1982

When the racehorse Shergar was kidnapped

11 February, 1983

"Leave the tea party, Mr Duffy! You're suffering from a dangerous outbreak of sanity..."

Mr Duffy, the leader of the Engineers' Union, did not like Labour's policy of unilateral disarmament

20 April, 1983

WALKS WITH THE DOG ON HAMPSTEAD HEATH, CONTINUED . . .

Enter Neil Kinnock, the new Leader of the Labour Party

4 December, 1983

Naturally, Mr Benn continues his policy of being a burden to the Party Leader

4 March, 1984

1 April, 1984

'Divided by the same language'

GOODNESS! THE NATO TROOPS ACTUALLY AGREE ABOUT SOMETHING—THEY LOVE THE SAME PIN-UP!

30 May, 1964

The Beatles sweep the world

23 September, 1964

"Mr. Nixon, it's immoral to defend far-away Asians against Communism, but never forget it's very moral to defend us Europeans in Europe against Communism"

Many Europeans criticised America for defending South Korea from the Communist invaders of North Korea

6 May, 1970

"Gee! I don't see what's so difficult about leaving someone alone!"

Senator Edward Kennedy accidentally drove his car off a bridge into the water with a woman friend. He escaped from the car and swam to safety. The girl was left in the car and drowned

22 October, 1971

'He that is without sin among you, let him first cast a stone . . .'
[St. John, Chapter 8, verse 7]

The Watergate affair begins to surface

2 May, 1973

"Ah! The President's acting fast to placate the black vote..."

17 August, 1979

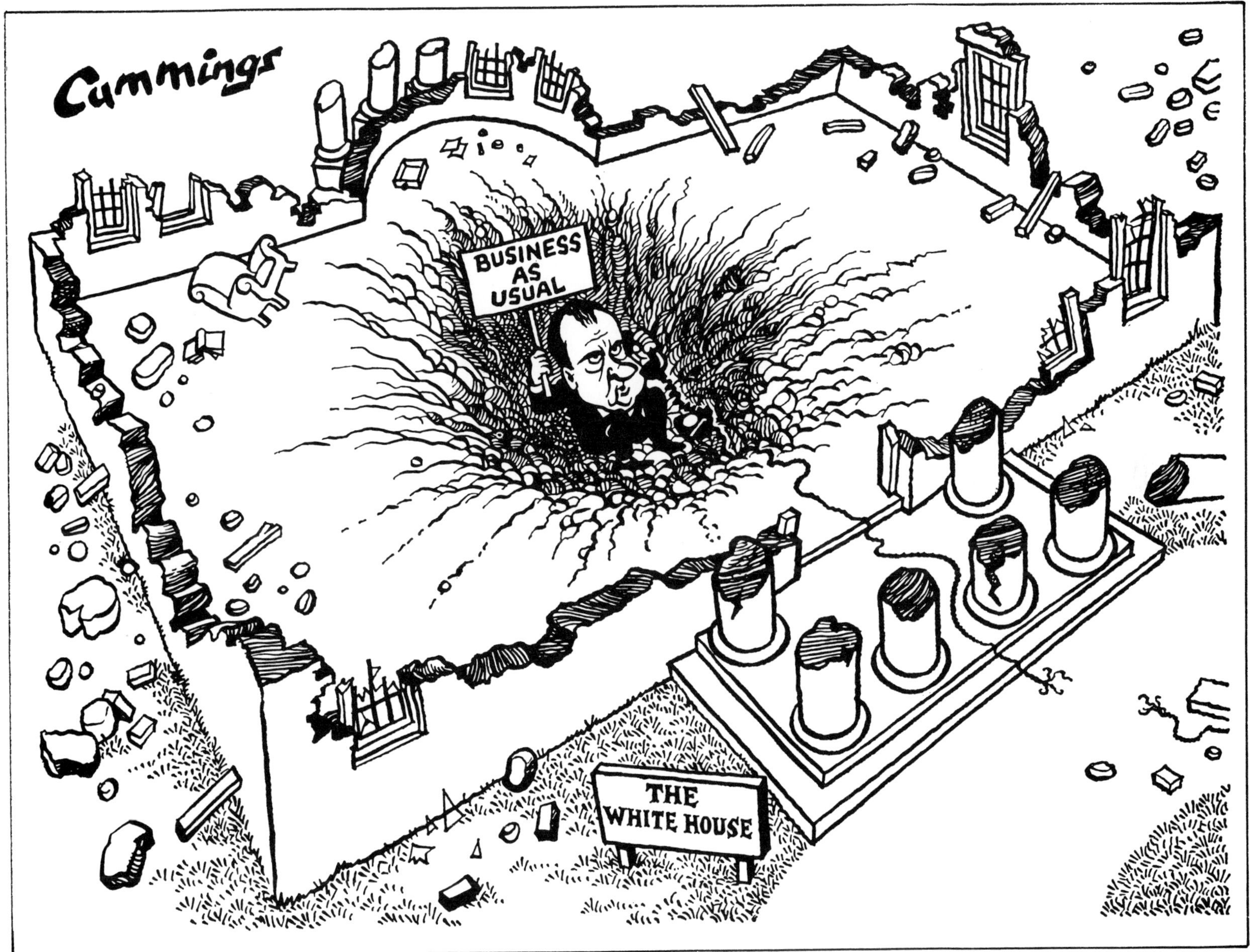

The Watergate affair rocks the White House

7 May, 1973

7 August, 1974

" ...and if I get elected President I shan't conduct business from THAT house of dubious repute

16 June, 1976

Everything goes wrong for America under Carter's presidency

3 November, 1978

"Advise me, Mr Nixon! I can't even sell a second-hand peanut!"

There was tremendous disillusion with the fumblings of President Carter

22 July, 1979

During the Falklands crisis Reagan's "even-handed" approach to the two sides infuriated the British

18 April, 1982

‘With love from Russia!’

IT'S SIMPLY A MATTER OF ARMBANDS

24 June, 1955

Gagarin and Titov, the Russian astronauts, make their epoch-making journey into space

14 August, 1961

"Instead of the usual trade supplies, Mao, you can have this load . . . as you're so keen on him!"

Krushchev denounces the memory of Stalin and maintains sour relations with China

13 November, 1961

Dealing with the Czech rebellion – the "Communist Spring"

24 July, 1968

Dr Kissinger does his best

7 March, 1976

16 April, 1978

"Lock out, Mr Brezhnev! That tough new Polish Pope is about to issue a Pastoral Message!"

18 October, 1978

LOCKING THE STABLE DOOR AFTER THE HORSE HAS BOLTED...

The world is too wicked a place for "born-again Christian" presidents like Carter to live in

11 January, 1980

"Mr Reagan! As soon as you're President, may we re-start SALT talks to curb the dangerous proliferation of Polish missiles?"

Solidarity and the Church fight Communist oppression in Poland

21 December, 1980

'Capitalism will make the noose for its own hanging" . . . Lenin

1 September, 1982

"Please do not be disturbed! The world is safely in the hands of the chaise longue and the bath chair!"

4 September, 1982

THE INHUMAN RACE

12 November, 1982

"It's maddening that we know nothing about the new Russian Pharaoh but he knows everything about us."

14 November, 1982

5 December, 1982

12 December, 1982

"Now we're safe! We only have to ask the wolf to sign the pledge to be a vegetarian, too!"

15 December, 1982

Cummings
THE DETERRENT THAT'S STOPPED WORLD WAR 3 BREAKING OUT FOR 38 YEARS
WAR

3 April, 1983

29 April, 1983

"Surprise! Surprise! King Kong is behaving exactly like King Kong!"

The Russians shoot down the Korean Airlines jumbo jet killing over two hundred people

4 September, 1983

"They're desperately trying to find a youthful image—someone as young as President Reagan"

20 November, 1983

'The Entente Discordiale'

"My dear Macmillan, what do you know about political constitutions—you just don't have our unrivalled experience!"

18 April, 1962

A view of Britain from the other side of the channel during the Profumo scandal

6 June, 1963

"I understand you! I'm still avenging the Battle of Waterloo!"

7 July, 1967

General de Gaulle made a visit to Quebec and encouraged the French Canadians to rejoin France

26 July, 1967

"Isn't it time, Mr. Kosygin, that we gave our man in Paris the Order of Lenin?"

24 November, 1967

"Take another train? But one day we might be allowed to ride on the engine!"

3 December, 1967

"Mon Dieu, Mme. Pompadour! The Deluge is coming while I'm still <u>here</u>!"

The French students riot in the streets of Paris

20 May, 1968

8 January, 1969

STUDY OF A TYPICAL FRENCH FAMILY HAVING ITS MORNING HATE . . .

19 February, 1969

With the retirement of de Gaulle, the way opens for Britain to join the Common Market

2 June, 1969

The British Socialists are beaten in the election by Mrs Thatcher, and on the other side of the Channel, French Socialism breaks down in dismay and disappointment

11 June, 1983

23 March, 1984

"It's disgraceful, Mme. Thatcher! Who do you think you are – you're behaving like a Frenchman!"

7 December, 1983

Cummings
DOWN WITH BRITISH LAMB!
BRITISH LAMB SHALL NOT PASS!
"We were lucky on D-Day—we only had to fight the German Army
— not the French farmers!"

6 June, 1984

'Abroad "I don't like abroad!" – George V'

19 November, 1961

"It's too risky, President Nasser! Maybe the Israelis are being supported by a force even more powerful than the Americans . . ."

President Nasser starts his disastrous campaign to crush Israel

29 May, 1967

"Any more for Russian Roulette?"

11 June, 1967

"Even though we've left him with only his sleeve, I'll bet he's got a card up it."

The Israeli's triumph over the Egyptian President Nasser **12 June, 1967**

The leader of North Vietnam makes a point

5 February, 1968

The British Raj colonises the Empire.

The Empire colonises the British Raj.

25 February, 1968

A bad year for leaders – from President Johnson on the left to Russian Prime Minister Kosygin on the right

22 May, 1968

"How frightful if peace breaks out in Vietnam before next weekend!"

The Vietnam war was a splendid excuse – like C.N.D. – for addicts of protest to spend an enjoyable week-end

21 October, 1968

"It's outrageous—our customers are using them!"

31 December, 1969

The battered Egyptian Nasser contemplates the confident Israeli

9 February, 1970

"Run for your life! There's a rumour that UNO is going to be saddled with the Ulster problem!"

16 August, 1970

" What was so marvellous about the rest of the British Commonwealth was that we could always leave it "

21 March, 1971

Idi Amin expels the Uganda Asians from Uganda
Dr Vorster was Prime Minister of South Africa where blacks, Asians and Whites lived according to the rules of Apartheid

7 August, 1972

Arab terrorists murder Israeli athletes at the Olympic Games **6 September, 1972**

"Maybe if we'd had a woman as President we'd have won the war in Vietnam."

29 October, 1973

"I think I preferred Enoch when he wanted to keep people OUT!"

21 April, 1974

BLACK MAN'S BURDEN WHITE MAN'S BURDEN

9 June, 1977

AT THE HOUR OF SUNSET THE FAITHFUL OF THE WEST BOW DOWN IN THE DIRECTION OF MECCA
—IN ORDER TO BE IN A POSITION TO RECEIVE A THUMPING KICK IN THE POSTERIOR...

Enter the Ayatollah of Iran

14 February, 1979

If there's one thing worse than a tyrant, it's a liberator...

14 March, 1979

5 August, 1979

"I only want to punish the Shah!"

7 November, 1979

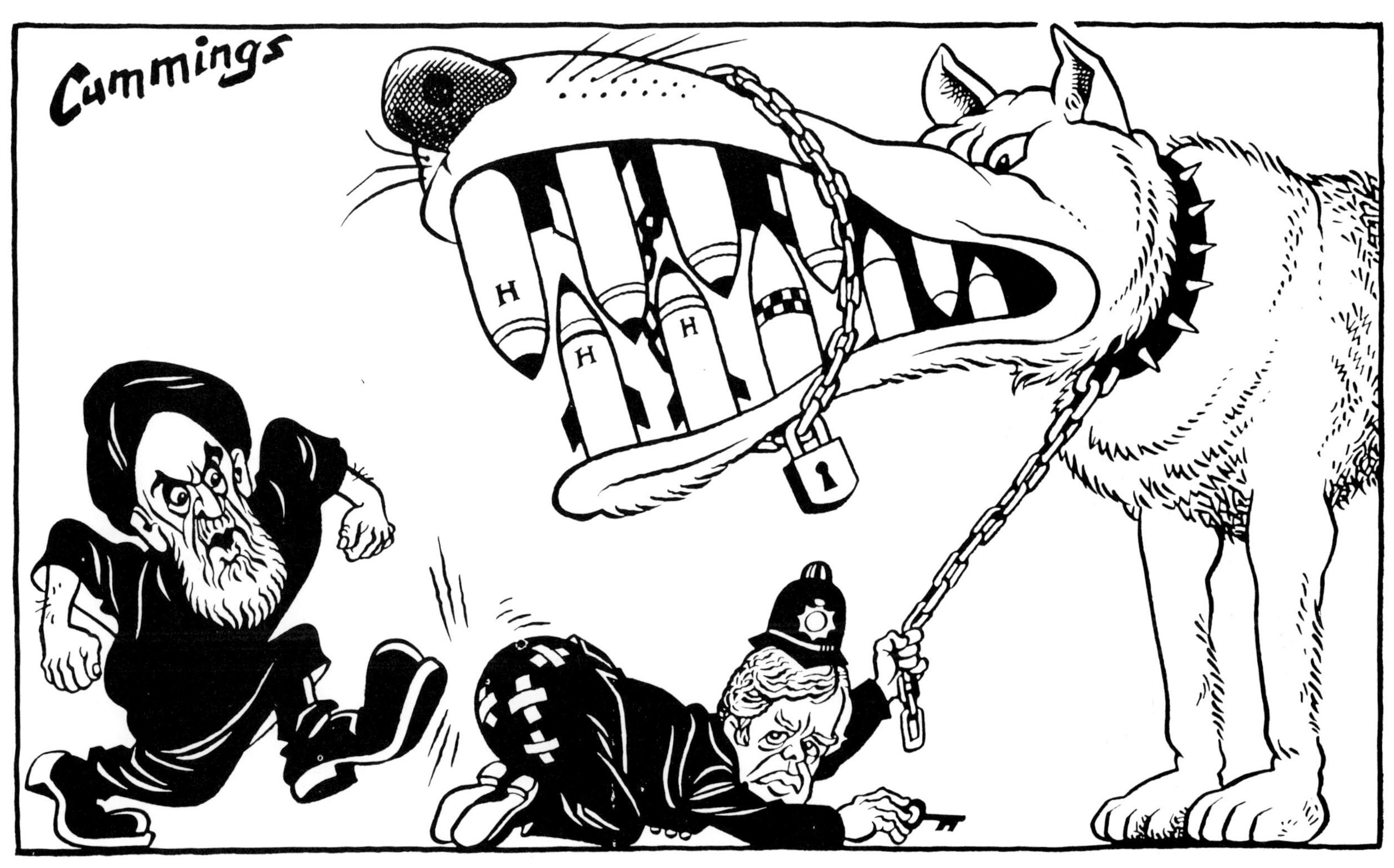

"There you go again, President Carter! Kicking my bovver boot with your bottom!"

9 April, 1980

"Congratulations, Mr Mugabe! I do hope this won't be another kiss of death!"

18 April, 1980

"The only solution to the Irish problem is to understand that no solution works"

24 October, 1982

27 April, 1984

American lawyers arrive in India to find clients among the victims to urge them to sue for damages against the chemical company

12 December, 1984

'The Permissive Society'

28 October, 1966

"A complaint has been made about you under the Race Relations Act. You're under arrest!"

14 August, 1967

Enoch Powell was attacked for his speech saying that immigration into Britain would cause grave problems – the so-called "rivers of blood" speech. Over two hundred letters from readers warmly approving this cartoon were sent to the cartoonist

22 April, 1968

Onassis marries Jacqueline Kennedy

20 October, 1968

23 December, 1968

14 February, 1976

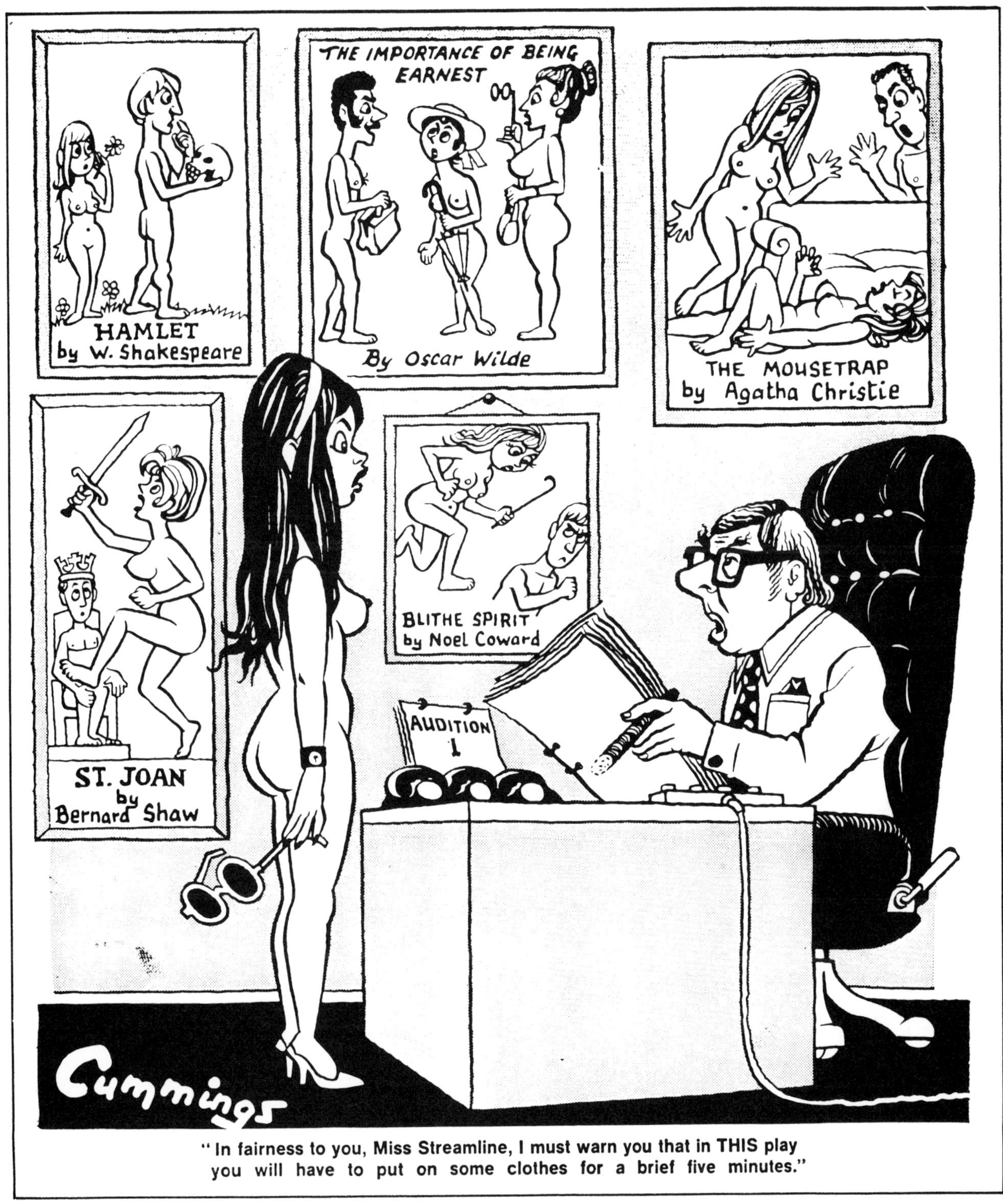

"In fairness to you, Miss Streamline, I must warn you that in THIS play you will have to put on some clothes for a brief five minutes."

With shows such as "Hair" and "Oh, Calcutta" nudity becomes fashionable

10 September, 1969

"Gee! Maybe it means we'll be raised to the status of women!"

28 August, 1970

A romantic and tender American film – 'Love Story' is a huge box office success

4 June, 1963

NOW THAT WOMEN'S LIB HAS DAWNED . . . by Cummings

"Young woman! Will you be able to keep my son in the manner to which he's been accustomed?"

"We've run out of petrol!"

"Caught you! With your secretary on your knee!"

"Why can't I have an E-Type Jaguar like Mr. Jones next door?„

"Darling! I'm expecting a happy event!"

10 February, 1973

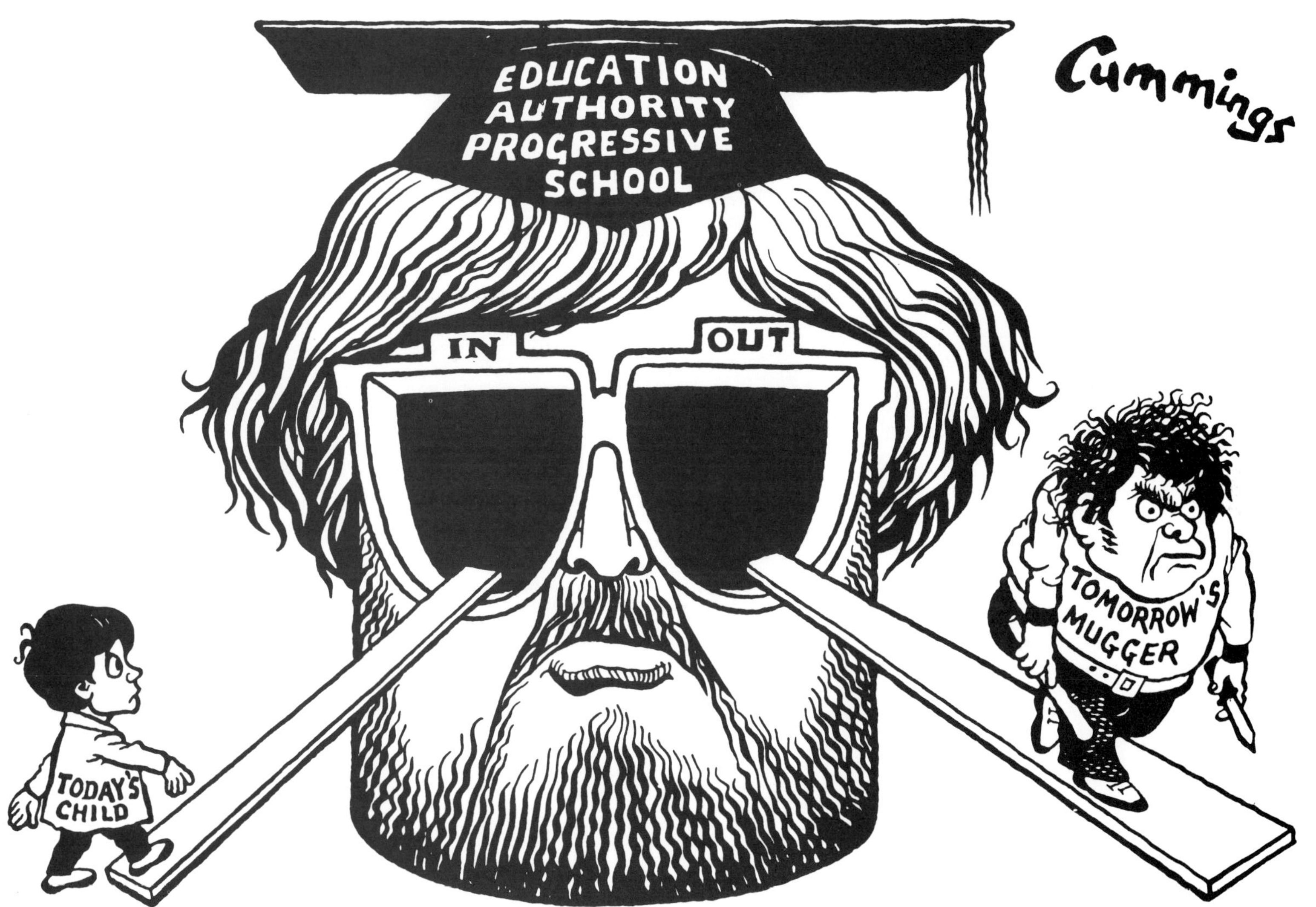

19 October, 1975

"Do you blame her? She must have heard that Lord Longford was going to visit her!"

13 September, 1977

"At long, long last, everybody is talking about the Liberal Party again"

7 February, 1978

"It's a pity Jeremy couldn't have disappeared like Stonehouse did..."

The Jeremy Thorpe court case arising from his relations with a man-friend, embarrasses the Liberal Party

17 September, 1978

"Phew! I hope I'll survive this terrifying storm in my tea cup!"

The scandal of traitor Anthony Blunt distracts the nation from the menaces of the Middle East

23 November, 1979

"There'd be less chance of starting World War Three if we stopped exporting sports and stuck to exporting arms!"

Wherever sport goes, the opposing fans riot

3 March, 1982

"Mugged? Cheer up, sir, I'll give your assailant a sharp tap on the head with the Scarman Report"

Lord Scarman wrote a report on the Brixton riots to improve relations between police and black people. By some it was unkindly called "The Muggers Charter"!

12 March, 1982

"Archbishop! The Devil is making a very attractive take-over bid for the Church of England!"

Elements in the Church were softening the tone of the Ten Commandments

21 August, 1982

"The Church of England, on the other hand, is plotting to assassinate itself!"

The Church starts to expound Labour's political ideas

5 January, 1983

"Just an Olde Englishe Ceremonial Custom, sir! Takes place every year—but it means nothing, of course"

26 June, 1983

"Your conduct is a disgrace! You don't eat your drugs for breakfast, you've failed your shoplifting exam, you wear a uniform, you call the teachers 'Sir' and you're STILL a virgin—you're expelled!".

"Trendy" schools go too far

31 August, 1983

"Excuse me—can you direct me to a church which preaches about Jesus Christ?"

22 April, 1984

‘Sea of Troubles’

General Election Day 1970

"The other Heads of State didn't dare leave home—they felt their jobs weren't secure enough . . ."

While Mr Obote, leader of Uganda, was at the Commonwealth Conference, he was ousted by Idi Amin who staged a military coup d'état

27 January, 1971

"I agree, cherie, that marriage is for keeps. But as it's a European marriage I must naturally be allowed to keep a mistress."

Common Market negotiations for Britain's entry suffered a hiccup because Heath wanted to maintain New Zealand's special commercial relations with Britain

21 May, 1971

"If this campaign doesn't sell the product then Tory Advertising Ltd. loses the British account!"

24 May, 1971

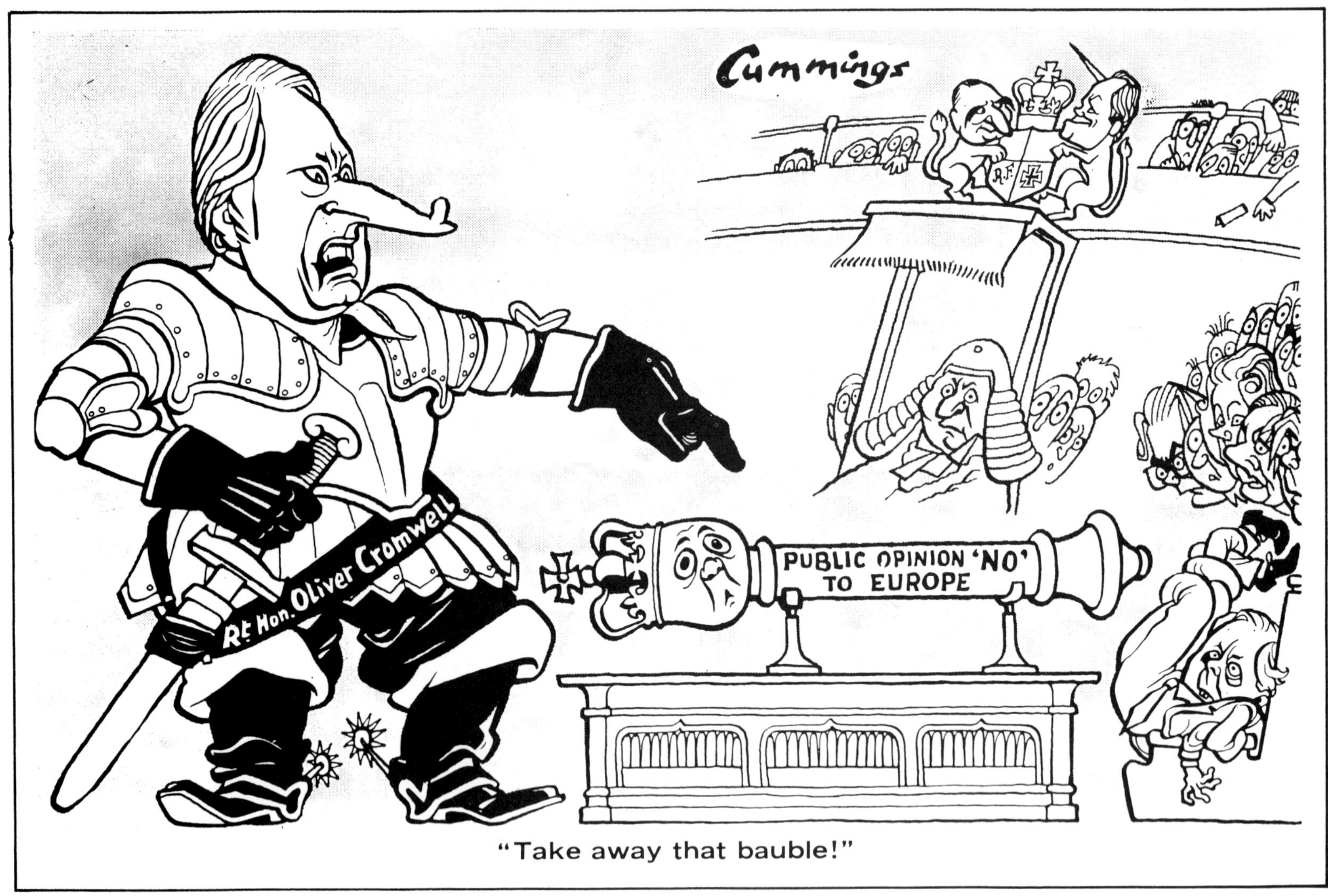

"Take away that bauble!"

At this period the British didn't like the idea of joining the Common Market

9 July, 1971

THE LEAGUE OF PURITY TRYING TO MAKE CASANOVA GIVE UP WOMEN...

Victor Feather, General Secretary of the T.U.C., surrounded by his favourite friends. He particularly liked this cartoon

28 February, 1972

"We can't have a referendum—it would go against our parliamentary traditions!"

19 March, 1972

Hugh Scanlon, the engineers union leader, Victor Feather, the T.U.C. General Secretary and Jack Jones, the transport union leader being beastly to Ted Heath

5 July, 1972

Trade union anarchy wanted to run the nation **31 July, 1972**

"I'm not a bachelor by choice, Jeremy! But the girl I want refused my flowers, my presents, my letters, and my invitations . . ."

26 February, 1973

"Top of the morning, gentlemen! I've brought you some grapes!"

By comparison with the agonies of Watergate, Nixon and the travails of some others, poor old Ted felt relatively healthy

8 June, 1973

"I had to say SOMETHING to remind everybody that I'M still awaiting the Call to save the nation . . ."

Lord Lambton and Earl Jellicoe were involved in one of those little Tory sex scandals which give such entertainment to the public and such embarrassment to sedate prime ministers

11 June, 1973

Heath calls the "Who Governs Britain?" General Election

8 February, 1974

"No thank you! I won't have anything to do with a 'ménage à trois'—it's immoral!"

Heath loses the election and tries to save the day by an alliance with the Liberals. The Liberals turn him down. Labour turns down an alliance with the Liberals

28 June, 1974

Disaffected Tory voters vote Liberal and thereby help Labour win the election of 1974

'Down Memory Lane'

While the colonies of the Empire wanted to run their own affairs, Britain was in charge of the Scots. Prime Minister, Foreign Secretary Home and Tory Party Chairman Macleod were all Scots

13 January, 1961

Things were not going very well, so Macmillan took punitive action to "encourage the others". This mass sacking was known as the "night of the long knives"

15 July, 1961

"It's all right for that bishop fellow not believing in the old image of God any more—but me, I'm beginning not to believe in Macmillan!"

The days of "they've never had it so good" seemed to be disappearing

30 March, 1963

June, 1963

In this drawing of John Profumo bewitched by the charms of Christine Keeler, the original drawing showed mermaid Keeler's breasts exposed in all their delightful glory. It is an interesting reflection on how times have changed since 1963, to recall that the Editor instructed me to cover her discreetly with her flowing hair so that public taste would not be outraged

"In response to the overwhelming popularity of the last number I shall now give an encore!"

As Prime Minister, Mr Macmillan did not enjoy the golden reverence and popularity now accorded to him as Lord Stockton, in sublime retirement as Elder Statesman

30 June, 1963

"It's all very well Maudling talking about youth, but I happen to be taking part in an X-certificate film..."

Macmillan is pursued by the Vassall and Philby spy scandals, the Keeler–Profumo affair, and the unlovely scent of landlord Rachman who used physical intimidation to evict tenants who were inconvenient

10 July, 1963

"Mr Scargill has broken into the Throne Room and is trying on Her Majesty's crown. Is there any law which allows us to remove him?"

"In view of the horrendous world he's just come into, it's amazing he looks so pleased."

"I'm deeply concerned about the problem of unemployment - the problem of one unemployed cabinet minister . . ."

"If I can't leave you for five minutes without you misbehaving, I shan't go abroad again!"

"It would do more for world peace if they abolished football."

"We may not be able to punish criminals, but we can jolly well punish their victims."

"God is very depressed today — the Church of England has just made Him redundant"

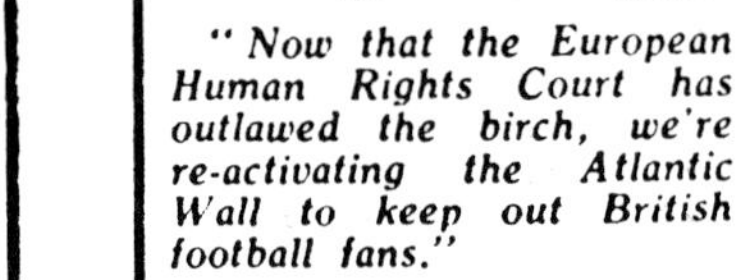

"Now that the European Human Rights Court has outlawed the birch, we're re-activating the Atlantic Wall to keep out British football fans."